MW00533660

# BAREFOOT

## Poems for Naked Feet

Stefi Weisburd

Illustrations by Lori McElrath-Eslick

WORDSONG

Honesdale, Pennsylvania

To Cass and Julian and their lively feet
—*S. W.*

To my brothers and sister,
Joel, Scott, Wendi:
our feet may be different sizes
but travel a similar path
—*L.M.E.*

Text copyright © 2008 by Stefi Weisburd
Illustrations copyright © 2008 by Lori McElrath-Eslick

The poem "Mountain Stream" first appeared in the July 2000 issue of *Cricket* magazine.
The poem "Feet of Engineering" first appeared in the April 2003 issue of *Cricket* magazine.

Wordsong
An Imprint of Boyds Mills Press, Inc.
815 Church Street
Honesdale, Pennsylvania 18431
Printed in China

Library of Congress Cataloging-in-Publication Data

Weisburd, Stefi.
  Barefoot : poems for naked feet / Stefi Weisburd ; illustrations by Lori McElrath-Eslick.
  p. cm.
ISBN-13: 978-1-59078-306-1 (alk. paper)
I. McElrath-Eslick, Lori, ill. II. Title.
PS3623.E43247B37 2007
811'.6—dc22
2006018011

First edition
The text of this book is set in 14-point Sabon.
The illustrations were done in watercolor.

10 9 8 7 6 5 4 3 2 1

# Table of Contents

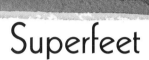

# Superfeet

Naturally
naked feet
don't need
superglue
or superheat

No supernatural
supersonic
supercharging
supertonic

Naturally
naked feet
are
entirely
complete

And with them a slider can

Spider-Man
like
slide
a
up
walk

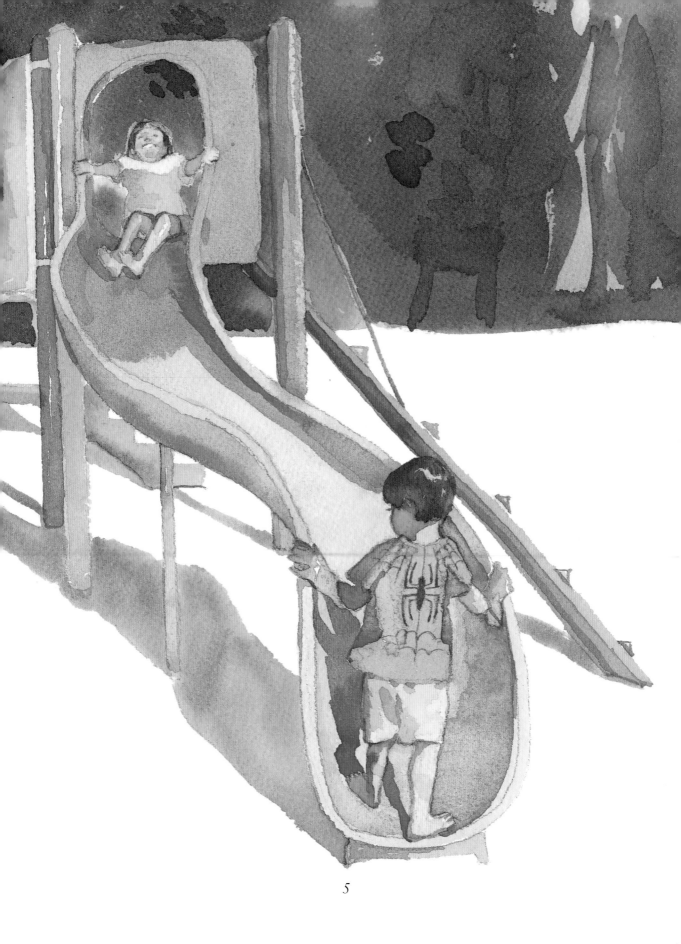

# That Picture

You weren't wearing shoes,
no shiny patent leather,
no fancy lace socks.
The photographer at J. C. Penney
wanted to hide your feet
under your skirt.
But I knew,
even though you couldn't walk yet,
your feet were ready
for adventure.
So when they blossomed
out from under your skirt,
we bought *that* picture.

# If

If I were a butterfly
my feet would taste flowers

    With toes of a gecko
    I'd climb up glass towers

Water strider's skates
would be quite appealing

    or a fly's Velcro grip
    to walk on the ceiling

With a cheetah's traction
I'd sprint stunning runs

    My elephant feet
    could hold up four tons

But I'd rather stay me
if I had to choose

    so you could still dance me
    while I stand on your shoes

# Shocking

Electric feet.
Plug 'em in,
rub electrons
off your skin.

Plow the rug.
You are exciting
your own private
bolts of lightning.

Is your brother
bugging you?
Want revenge?
What to do?

Rub your feet.
Target locked.
Charge! Discharge:
brother shocked.

# Godzilla at Her Sister's Birthday Party

*Crackle!*
   *Crinkle!*
        *Crunch!*

I march
   through the land
       of rumpled wrapping paper,
           punting hills of purple bows.

Stomping toward the city,
   I rumble, I roar,
       scattering fields of butterflies
           and herds of dinosaurs.

I tangle highways of ribbon,
   tumble skyscraper cards,
       terrifying the Barbie townsfolk
           sunbathing in yards.

Then I imagine *my* birthday has come.
   I kick up a yellow balloon,
       launching the sun.

# Vacant Houses

High heels
      cliff-side beauty on stilts
      toes might be cramped in the tiny basement

Flip-flops
      great lakefront property
      a drummer lives downstairs
      so be prepared for swacking sounds

Sister's pumps
      pretty decor, new glossy finish
      might not want to risk the high rental charges

Soccer cleats
      very cozy
      hot, humid, and stuffy three times a week
      foundation a bit rickety

Sandals
      good view of the stars
      not for the shy—no window shades
      residents may get tan lines

Boots
    sturdy brown brownstone
    but lack of skylights makes it dark and gloomy

Dog-stolen old sneaker
    fixer-upper
    extensive saliva damage

Slippers
    soft, luxurious carpeting
    flimsy doors, not recommended for
    cartwheelers or trampoline jumpers

Dad's shoes
    lots of room to roam
    in fact, too much square footage
    but the floors are worn smooth as marble
    feels like home

# Morning Chores for Feet

1. Comb the grass.

2. Dress in dew glitter and dandelion hats.

3. Patrol for new neighbors, mushrooms that moved in overnight.

4. Listen to the ground for the stirrings of earthworm gossip.

5. Feel the patio bricks gathering the sun's warm hellos.

6. Gently pet cat sprawled on patio bricks as she tries to hog the sun's warm hellos.

7. Get up on tiptoe so nose may smell a blossom.

8. Stand in a puddle and reflect.

9. Launch body into a somersault.

10. Lie body on its back, lift legs to hold up the sky and keep the clouds from falling.

Ah, the first day of summer vacation.

# Gardening

I plant myself
in flower pose.
In fragrant earth
I burrow toes.
My face tastes sun
and brims with light.
Arms entwine
the trellis tight.
Fingers sprout,
elbows thorn.
Look at me!
A rose is born.

!
k
w
a
h

in

*good-bye*

saying

me

That's

squawk?

to bust      that

thrust gravity's      hear

the      pull,      you

bounce      give me      the jolt      Did

this    or maybe   will      to burst    Hey!

Maybe     the next      into sky.

# Trampoline

# In Step

Foot **print** print print
The paint starts **bold,**
then fades to hint.

In soleful blues, toed greens,
leap-up yellows,
I paint a scene.

I make stars,
I stamp trees,
but mostly I print
crowds of me.

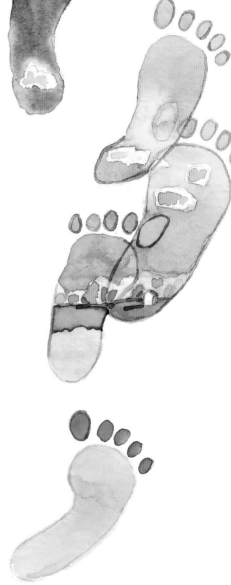

me me me me me me me me me me me me

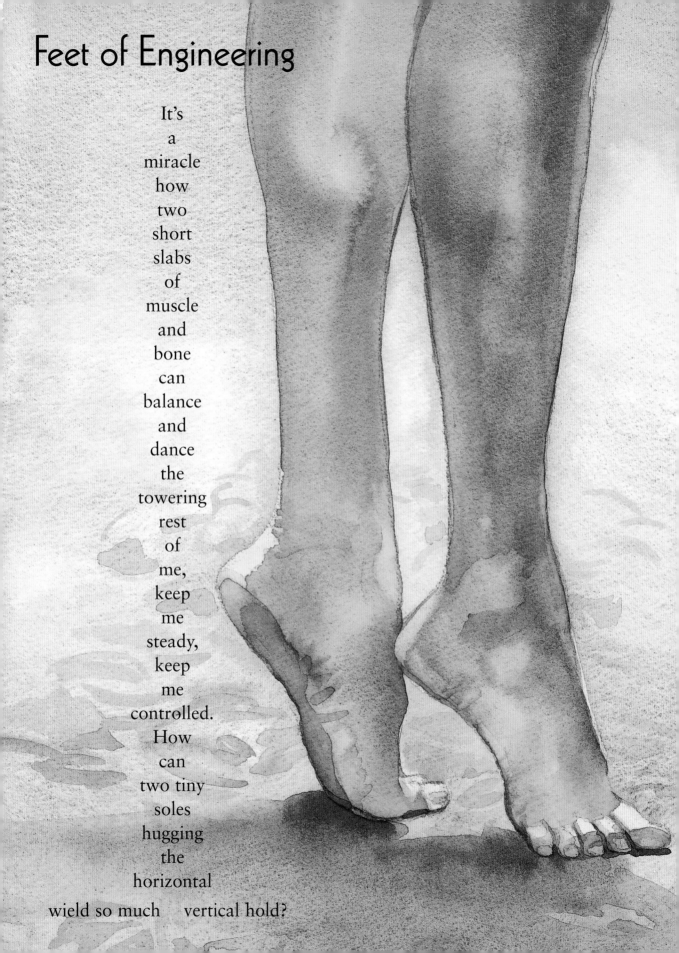

# Feet of Engineering

It's
a
miracle
how
two
short
slabs
of
muscle
and
bone
can
balance
and
dance
the
towering
rest
of
me,
keep
me
steady,
keep
me
controlled.
How
can
two tiny
soles
hugging
the
horizontal
wield so much    vertical hold?

# Wall Walkers

From up here we can see

Mrs. Vento's hubcap collection,
Sarah's sister putting zit gunk on her pimples,
Mr. Moss's little yap dogs *yap-yap-yapping* at us,
Noah making muscles in the mirror,
two squirrels stealing Dr. Righter's birdseed and gloating.

To see the whole world,
to see it all,

walk on a wall.

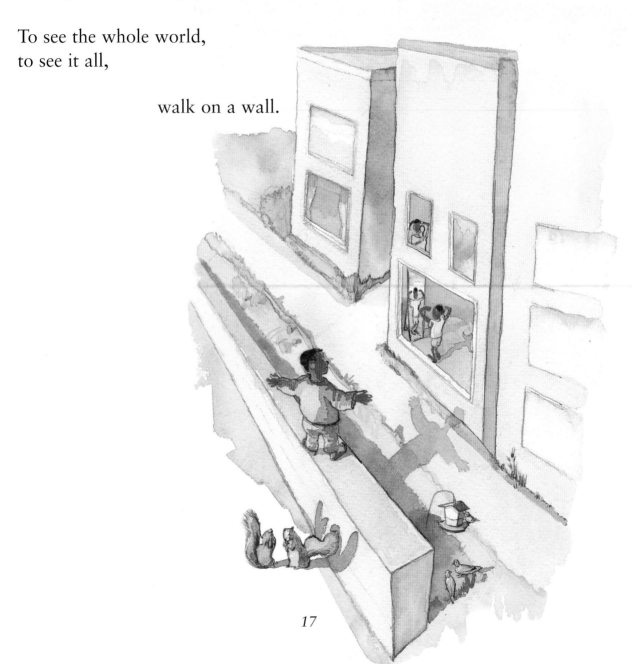

# What's Afoot at the Beach

Hot! Hot! Hot!
I try ballerina toes,
quick-stepping heels;
I try to imagine ice,
but nothing douses
the sand's
firecracker spice!

Bulldozer feet
crack
the salty crust,
plow roads,
pave
muddy mortar
and unearth
a quarter.

Some waves
are shy,
they whisper
foam *hellos*.
Some waves
are brash,
they spray
and thunder me
and, chuckling,
steal the sand
from under me.

Sea glass
        and shell hunts,
sandpipers bobbing,
        but nothing's quite
so satisfying
        as stepping on
slick seaweed and
        hearing the crisp, wet snap
that comes from popping
        the sea's bubble wrap.

# Hotel
# Swimming Pool's
# Evening Lament

I've been
so bored
staring
at the sky
all day
while you
were at
the beach
playing
with the ocean.
No one to swirl me.
No one to splash, to dive.
No one to swim through me sleek
and slow. Come on, child. At least dip in a        toe.

# Jacuzzi Jet

A Jacuzzi jet
is writing
*urgentnotesonthebottomofmyfoot*

It  r u s h e  s
torrents of worried words
dots every *i*
crosses every *t*
sends me
whirlpools of commas

I wish I were fluent in water
then I'd know
what in the world the bubbles
     are  b  ᵃ  b  b  ˡ  ᵢ  n  ᵍ

# Bathtub

two puckered old men
splash out and totter
trailing beards of water
I almost don't recognize
my toes
in disguise
squinting at me
with Grandpa's eyes

# A Ride in the Country

Foot!
Want to go for a drive?
Want to *go go go*?
Hang your head out
the car *WIND*ow?

Toes:   Pant, lick at air.
Heel:  Sniff   Snort   SNEEZE!

I can see your
imaginary fur
flung by breeze,
your dark eyes
riveted
on the speeding view.

Go on, boy!
Growl at birds,
bark at herds of moo.
Someday Dad
will let me
have a real dog, too.

# Camping

It's too cold to send
my freezing feet to
Antarctica at the bottom
of my sleeping bag

Dad pulls off my socks
and wraps my feet under
his shirt against his warm chest

This is better than roasting marshmallows

# Mountain Stream

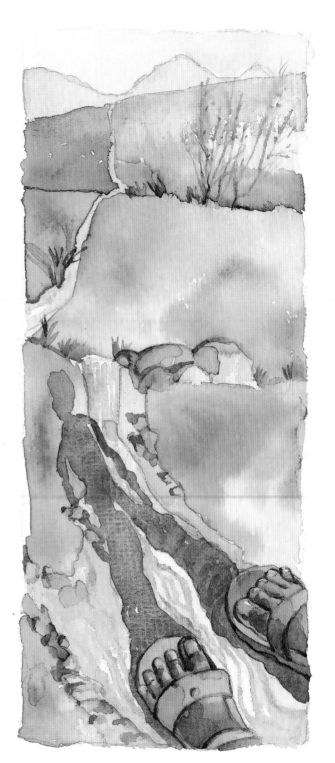

even in July
the stones
huddle
in green shawls of algae

the pussy willows
are busy knitting mittens

water glitters
with a blizzard of light

my body is sweltering with summer
but even in July
my icy feet know
the mountain
is thinking *snow*

# Snake Fight

Sneaking,
sliding,
slithering
up
my best
friend's
shin.

Now
his
is
twining,
climbing,
quivering
my skin.

Our feet flex,
our feet sway,
heels hover,
toes splay.

Now attack!
Quick strike!
Toes jab,
toenails bite.

There's not one
smirk
or hiss
or jiggle,
not one jerk
or flick
or giggle.

Hardly a hint
above the table
where dinner steams,
serene and stable.
Yet Mama smiles,
"Boys, eat some more
and put those snakes
back on the floor."

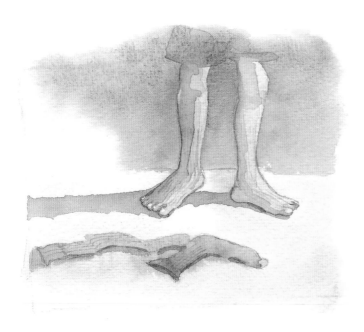

# Shoe Tattoo

Tight shoes,
ribbed socks,
leave lines
embossed.
Streams and hills,
fields of wheat.
A tiny landscape
on my feet!

# Love Tip No. 3

Who sent Brett this valentine?
I bet he'll never know.
When I signed his valentine
the pen was between my toes.

# Mama

When she
comes home
from work
tired
tired
I rub her feet
especially
the little toes.
Her nail polish
is chipped.
She says only I
know how to get
the river running again
in her bones.

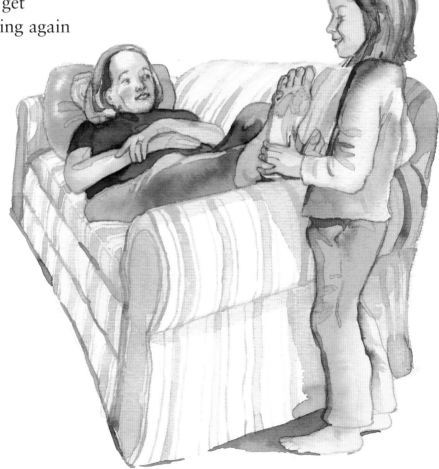

# Saturday Night

My babysitter's hair
smells of coconut. Her earrings
tinkle like chandeliers,
and in her purse are
ten tiny, shiny bottles—Lilac Ice,
Chocolate Shake, Hot Fuchsia . . .
"*Let's paint your nails*," she says.
I can't choose just one color,
so she gives each toe
its own makeover: Four-Alarm Red
for the big left toe that got stubbed,
Peach Blush for the shiest little toe . . .
When she's done, it's simply *divine*, darling,
each toe dressed in its own satin gown,
ready to walk into a fairy tale.

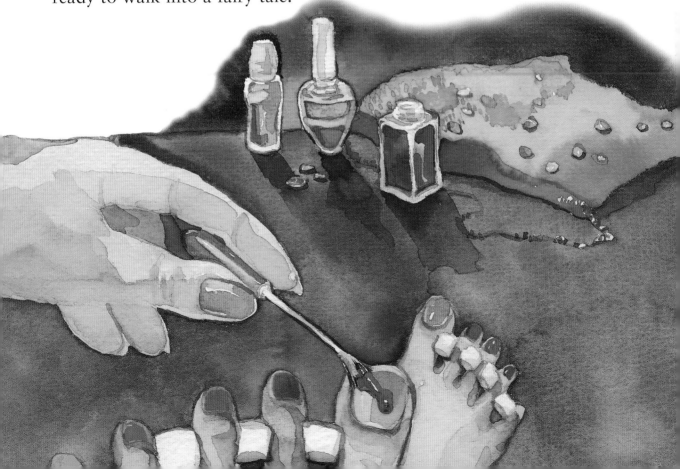

# Mehndi Party

Before cousin Anisha
gets married, we'll eat sweets
and sing all afternoon while *mehndi* artists
paint our hands and feet
with a cool red paste
made from henna leaves.

My aunties' feet will be traced
with swirls and paisleys, Mom's
with flowers and vines, lacy patterns,
delicate lines. I'm going to ask
for tiny wings hidden in the henna.
Then tonight when I fall into my dreams
my feet will take me

flying.

# Dusk

When the sun's a mere yolk
about to drop
from the horizon,

      step off
the sidewalk that's still
heckling everyone with *hot!*

Step onto
      a cool green whisper—
          the lawn's long exhale,
like fresh, chilled silk
      streaming up your ankles.

The grass has waited this whole
sticky, summer-swollen day
      for the company of your
feet running and twirling,

      waited to feel you cartwheel:

palm ponytail palm foot foot palm ponytail palm foot foot

as you spoke your legs across the cool moon

and the crickets applaud.

# Warning Label

rosebush thorns
doggy poo
igloo ice
superglue
athlete's fungus
scalding lava
porcupines
steaming java
hungry sharks
red-hot coals
fire sparks
deep dark holes
tacks and jacks
piles of screws
someone's spit
gum (well chewed)
stinging bees
spiked high heels
endless tickles
careless wheels

To all owners:
Beware! Retreat
from these hazards
to your bare feet.